Worship

Discovering What Scripture Says

LARRY SIBLEY

SHAW BOOKS

an imprint of WATERBROOK PRESS

Worship

A SHAW BOOK

PUBLISHED BY WATERBROOK PRESS

2375 Telstar Drive, Suite 160

Colorado Springs, Colorado 80920

A division of Random House, Inc.

All Scripture quotations, unless otherwise indicated, are taken from the *Holy Bible, New International Version*®. NIV®. Copyright © 1973, 1978, 1984 by International Bible Society. Used by permission of Zondervan Publishing House. All rights reserved.

ISBN 0-87788-911-2

SHAW BOOKS and its aspen leaf logo are trademarks of WaterBrook Press, a division of Random House, Inc.

Printed in the United States of America

2001

10 9 8 7 6 5 4 3 2 1

Contents

How to Use This Studyguide

isherman studyguides are based on the inductive approach to Bible study. Inductive study is discovery study; we discover what the Bible says as we ask questions about its content and search for answers. This is quite different from the process in which a teacher *tells* a group *about* the Bible—what it means and what to do about it. In inductive study God speaks directly to each of us through his Word.

A group functions best when a leader keeps the discussion on target, but the leader is neither the teacher nor the "answer person." A leader's responsibility is to *ask*—not *tell*. The answers come from the text itself as group members examine, discuss, and think together about the passage.

There are four kinds of questions in each study. The first is an *approach question.* Asked and answered before the Bible passage is read, this question breaks the ice and helps you start thinking about the topic of the Bible study. It begins to reveal where thoughts and feelings need to be transformed by Scripture.

Some of the early questions in each study are *observation questions*—who, what, where, when, and how—designed to help you learn some basic facts about the passage of Scripture.

Once you know what the Bible says, you then need to ask, *What does it mean?* These *interpretation questions* help you to discover the writer's basic message.

Next come *application questions,* which ask, *What does it mean to me?* They challenge you to live out the Scripture's life-transforming message.

Fisherman studyguides provide spaces between questions for jotting down responses as well as any related questions you would like to raise in the group. Each group member should have a copy of the studyguide and may take a turn in leading the group.

A group should use any accurate, modern translation of the Bible such as the *New International Version,* the *New American Standard Bible,* the *New Revised Standard Version,* the *New Jerusalem Bible,* or the *Good News Bible.* (Other translations or paraphrases of the Bible may be referred to when additional help is needed.) Bible commentaries should not be brought to a Bible study because they tend to dampen discussion and keep people from thinking for themselves.

SUGGESTIONS FOR GROUP LEADERS

1. Thoroughly read and study the Bible passage before the meeting. Get a firm grasp on its themes and begin applying its teachings for yourself. Pray that the Holy Spirit will "guide you into all truth" (John 16:13) so that your leadership will guide others.

2. If any of the studyguide's questions seem ambiguous or unnatural to you, rephrase them, feeling free to add others that seem necessary to bring out the meaning of a verse.

3. Begin (and end) the study promptly. Start by asking someone to pray that every participant will both understand the passage and be open to its transforming power. Remember, the Holy Spirit is the teacher, not you!

4. Ask for volunteers to read the passages aloud.

5. As you ask the studyguide's questions in sequence, encourage everyone to participate in the discussion. If some are silent, try gently suggesting, "Let's have an answer from someone who hasn't spoken up yet."

6. If a question comes up that you can't answer, don't be afraid to admit that you're baffled. Assign the topic as a research project for someone to report on next week, or say, "I'll do some studying and let you know what I find out."

7. Keep the discussion moving, but be sure it stays focused. Though a certain number of tangents are inevitable, you'll want to quickly bring the discussion back to the topic at hand. Also, learn to pace the discussion so that you finish the lesson in the time allotted.

8. Don't be afraid of silences; some questions take time to answer, and some people need time to gather courage to speak. If silence persists, rephrase your question, but resist the temptation to answer it yourself.

9. If someone comes up with an answer that is clearly illogical or unbiblical, ask for further clarification: "What verse suggests that to you?"

10. Discourage overuse of cross references. Learn all you can from the passage at hand, while selectively incorporating a few important references suggested in the studyguide.

11. Some questions are marked with a ✐. This indicates that further information is available in the Leader's Notes at the back of the guide.

12. For further information on getting a new Bible
   study group started and keeping it functioning
   effectively, read *You Can Start a Bible Study Group*
   by Gladys Hunt and *Pilgrims in Progress: Growing
   Through Groups* by Jim and Carol Plueddemann.
   (Both books are available from Shaw Books.)

S UGGESTIONS FOR G ROUP M EMBERS

1. Learn and apply the following ground rules for
   effective Bible study. (If new members join the
   group later, review these guidelines with the whole
   group.)
2. Remember that your goal is to learn all that you can
   from the Bible passage being studied. Let it speak for
   itself without using Bible commentaries or other
   Bible passages. There is more than enough in each
   assigned passage to keep your group productively
   occupied for one session. Sticking to the passage
   saves the group from insecurity ("I don't have the
   right reference books—or the time to read anything
   else.") and confusion ("Where did that come from?
   I thought we were studying _____.").
3. Avoid the temptation to bring up those fascinating
   tangents that don't really grow out of the passage
   you are discussing. If the topic is of common interest, you can bring it up later in informal conversa-
   tion after the study. Meanwhile, help one another
   stick to the subject.
4. Encourage one another to participate. People remember best what they discover and verbalize for

themselves. Some people are naturally shy, while others may be afraid of making a mistake. If your discussion is free and friendly and you show real interest in what group members think and feel, the quieter ones will be more likely to speak up. Remember, the more people involved in a discussion, the richer it will be.

5. Guard yourself from answering too many questions or talking too much. Give others a chance to share their ideas. If you are one who participates easily, discipline yourself by counting to ten before you open your mouth.

6. Make personal, honest applications and commit yourself to letting God's Word change you.

Discovering What Scripture Says

Worship is a basic—though often elusive—element of our faith. What exactly is worship, and how are we to enter God's presence?

The Bible is full of clues about worship, as well as passages that teach about it directly. This guide will focus on stories of people who worshiped in God's presence. As we watch these people worship and join them in worship, we'll begin to understand what God desires from us. We'll see from their examples how to live out the scriptural commands and teachings about entering God's presence.

We'll join Abraham as he prays under a lonely tree, hear God's word from Moses, rejoice in procession with David, cry out in pain and praise with the psalmist, welcome children as they come to Jesus, bless God in prayer with Paul, and enter heaven with John.

We'll use our senses as we hear songs, cymbals, and drums; feel the person next to us at God's Communion table; see the world at praise; and taste how good God is. We'll learn the hows and whys of singing, praying, and listening, and we'll watch individuals, crowds, and families as they worship. We'll worship God with our entire souls and bodies; we'll enjoy his presence.

Historically, the Psalms have been the prayer and worship book of the church. They teach us the vocabulary of worship, the language of the heavenly country to which we belong. The Psalms assure us that both our pain and our gratitude are welcome sounds to God's ears, and we will come back to these songs again and again.

In an appendix at the back of this guide you will find a suggested seven-week reading plan for the Psalms. Using this guide is one way you can enrich your own personal worship. Read and meditate on the psalms listed, and use them to guide your praying.

As we put the pieces of worship together, we'll discover that they lead us into the heavens to take our seat with Christ at God's side.

> Just as with a gift given to a friend:
>> something loved, cherished, appreciated (a coffee
>> mug or vase that sat on my shelf; a plant I raised
>> myself);
> So this service is offered to God for his pleasure
>> (carefully chosen words, tunes, harmonies, move-
>> ments, fragrances).
> Our pleasure (which notices the beauty of holiness, if only
> passing) is in anticipating his—
>> somehow knowing he delights (we offer by faith,
>> not by sight) because we've done what he said he
>> wants.

Praising God, Our Divine Warrior

PSALM 68

The most valuable thing the Psalms do for me is to express that same delight in God which made David dance.... [Compared] with the merely dutiful "church-going" and laborious "saying our prayers" to which most of us are...often reduced...it stands out as something astonishingly robust, virile and spontaneous.

—C. S. LEWIS, *Reflections on the Psalms*

Worship is a personal expression of love and thanks to our worthy God. Whether or not we feel the freedom to dance before God, as David did in the Old Testament account, each of us can celebrate God's greatness with renewed vigor as we see more of who he is. In this poetic account of an ancient Hebrew service, we will identify some basic elements of worship and gain new insights into God's awesome power and might.

1. Think about a recent church service you attended. Which of your five senses (hearing, seeing, feeling, tasting, smelling) were involved in praising God?

Read Psalm 68:1-10.

✍ 2. Describe God's actions in verses 6-10. Who is affected by these actions?

✍ 3. What contrasts do you see between the groups of people mentioned in verses 1-3 and 5-10? Describe the connection between the defeat of God's enemies and the blessings he gives to his poor and needy people.

4. What events in your recent experience show God defeating his enemies and blessing the poor and needy? Which elements in a worship service could be used to praise him for these actions?

READ PSALM 68:11-27.

⚔ 5. Describe what God has done for his people. Which elements of a modern worship service might correspond to this recital of God's victories?

⚔ 6. How do God's people respond to the record of his works (verses 19-20)? What elements of your church's worship service are like this?

7. Describe the scene that you find in verses 24-27.
    Imagine yourself as one of the participants. Which
    of your senses would be involved?

8. Describe how your church uses the gathering
    process (including a procession, if there is one) as
    a way of celebrating God's victories and blessings
    of the previous week?

READ PSALM 68:28-35.

9. Who is speaking in these verses as the scene shifts?
    Who is being spoken to? What element of worship
    do you find here?

10. Who is the focus of these final verses? What qualities of God are proclaimed?

11. Reread the psalm and find as many names or descriptive titles for God as you can. How does this consistently varied mention of him provide a focus for worship?

12. List all the elements of worship found in this psalm, in the order that they appear. Compare this with the order of worship at your church. What similarities or differences do you see?

13. Give one example of how God is at work in your life, then prayerfully give him thanks and praise. You might use Psalm 136 as a model to guide your prayer. After each example of God's active presence, include the refrain, "His love endures forever."

Abram's Altars

GENESIS 12:1-9; 13:1-4,18; EXODUS 40

*To live a spiritual life we must first find the
courage to enter into the desert of our loneliness
and to change it by gentle and persistent efforts
into a garden of solitude.*

—HENRI NOUWEN, *Reaching Out*

All of us can recall times when we have felt the pain of acute loneliness. To escape the pain we may have buried ourselves in our work, gone to countless parties, or watched television nonstop. But Abram found that as he worshiped God in deserted places, these lonely times of his life were filled with rich promise because God met him there.

1. Briefly describe a recent time of solitude with God. Was it like a garden or like a desert? Why?

READ GENESIS 12:1-9.

⚲ 2. Why did Abram leave his home? Who went with him? What did God promise in verses 2-3?

⚲ 3. What does the text tell you about each place Abram stayed? Imagine yourself as Abram in a new land. How would you feel?

⚲ 4. In verse 7 what did God add to his previous promise? Compare the way God communicated with Abram in verse 1 and verse 7.

5. When Abram reached Bethel, what was different about the setting? What actions did Abram repeat here? What new action is mentioned?

6. Compare the meaning of "pitched his tent" with "built an altar" in Genesis 12:8. Which has more significance or permanence in your life: the buildings in which you live and work or your worship?

7. What are some special places that seem God-filled to you? Describe one of these places.

READ GENESIS 13:1-4,18.

8. As Abram returned to Bethel and moved to
    Hebron, what actions did he repeat?

9. After Abram left each place, what did he leave
    behind to show he had been there?

10. What lessons about God's character and about wor-
    ship can you draw from Abram's example?

READ EXODUS 40.

11. Compare the worship in this setting with Abram's
    worship experiences in the previous passages. What
    differences do you notice?

12. Our worship times today are sometimes complex, sometimes simple. What elements are common to both types of worship?

13. Identify one solitary place you can go this week for time alone with God. What can you do to "call on the Lord" as Abram did?

STUDY 3

The Word of the Lord

DEUTERONOMY 6:1-9,20-25; 31:9-13

It is a great thing, this reading of the Scriptures. For it is not possible ever to exhaust the mind of the Scriptures. It is a well that has no bottom.

—JOHN CHRYSOSTOM, A.D. 398–407

When I was a toddler, my parents used to read and sing to me in a special rocking chair. I still remember some of the stories and songs, although I haven't heard them for years. I also remember my father and grandfather reading aloud from the Bible at home and at church. Recently I've been listening to Scripture in church with my Bible closed, learning again to *hear* God's Word. The readings are making a deeper impression because I am *listening*.

1. What is your earliest memory of being read to at home? in church?

Read Deuteronomy 6:1-9,20-25.

2. According to Moses, who is the ultimate source of the commands, decrees, and laws he taught to Israel (verse 1)? What does Moses' statement imply about all five books of the Law—and the rest of the Bible?

3. What was God's purpose in giving these commandments (verses 2-3)? What was Israel's part in fulfilling this purpose?

4. According to verses 6-9, what are parents instructed to do? What truths about God are they to teach their children (verses 3-5)?

5. What childhood memories do you have of conversations about God? What was your image or concept of God at that time?

6. What other aspect of home life is mentioned in verse 20? What questions do you remember asking as a child? Who answered them best?

READ DEUTERONOMY 31:9-13.

7. What two things did Moses do in verse 9? How has this helped the generations of believers who followed him?

✐ 8. In verses 10-11, what did Moses command the priests and elders of Israel to do? How would this command differ from the daily conversations of the home?

9. What reason did Moses give for the public readings of God's commandments (verses 12-13)?

✐ 10. How would this public reading—along with conversations in the home—have reinforced and completed the process of instructing the people, especially the children? How do Bible readings in worship services today have a similar effect?

11. In later years the Levites explained the meaning of the readings from the Law to the Israelites. In what ways does an explanation (sermon) help us understand and obey God's Word or strengthen our worship?

12. When we listen carefully to a friend or parent, we are showing that we respect (fear) them. How is it an act of worship to carefully listen to the private reading of God's Word at home and public readings at church?

Worshiping When We Hurt

PSALM 102:1-22

When the godly weep, they weep unto God,
and weeping before God is worship as
much as rejoicing before God.

—HUGHES OLIPHANT OLD

Themes and Variations for a Christian Doxology

It seems that church is the last place we want to go when we are down or not feeling "all together." But according to this psalm, that's the very time we can freely and fearlessly meet with God. Turning to God in our suffering is an act of faith and can renew us even in the midst of our tears.

1. Are there times when you don't "feel like church" or are too sad to worship? How do you deal with these situations?

READ PSALM 102:1-7.

2. What different phrases does the author use in verses 1-2 to describe his feelings and desires?

3. To what did the psalmist compare himself in verses 3-7? What do these things have in common?

4. How would you summarize the psalmist's feelings in these verses?

5. Describe a situation when you have felt time was running out or you were very lonely. What figure of speech might describe your feelings in that situation?

READ PSALM 102:8-10.

6. What reason did the psalmist give for his plight? How do verses 8-9 help explain the taunts of his enemies?

7. What deeper reason did the psalmist offer for his troubles in verse 10? When you have felt abandoned by God or subject to his wrath, who took advantage of your vulnerability? who encouraged you?

8. How might parts of this psalm be used in a worship service to express feelings of being abandoned by God? Paraphrase the psalm to use during your own personal time with God.

READ PSALM 102:11-22.

9. What images did the psalmist use to contrast God with himself (verses 11-17)? What did he say about God's attitude toward Zion and toward his people?

10. What hope did the psalmist express in verse 17? How does this hope speak to the needs that were expressed in verses 3-11? How does this encourage you to worship by weeping?

11. What impact will answered prayer in the life of the psalmist have on future generations (verses 18-20)? on the peoples of the earth (verses 21-22)?

12. In light of what you have discovered in this psalm, how can "weeping before God" ultimately lead to "rejoicing before God"?

Psalm Praise

PSALM 66; 145:1-12

*We delight to praise what we enjoy, because the praise
not merely expresses but completes the enjoyment.*
—C. S. LEWIS, *Reflections on the Psalms*

A t times our worship can suffer from our short memories. "What do I have to praise God for?" we may ask. We need to remember what God has done for us and those things we can genuinely and joyfully give thanks for.

1. Briefly describe an occasion when you thanked a friend or praised someone quite spontaneously. What motivated you to verbally express your thanks or praise?

READ PSALM 66:1-12.

2. What words or phrases express worship in verses
   1-4? How are the commands of verses 1-3a fulfilled
   in verses 3b-4?

☞ 3. How is our gratitude made complete when we sing
   praise, shout our thanks, or bow down before God?

☞ 4. To what great event in Israel's history are verses 5-12
   referring? Why was this event so important to Israel?

READ PSALM 66:13-20.

5. In what ways did the psalmist express his thanks in verses 13-15?

6. Verses 16-20 describe an event in the life of the psalmist. As you compare this event with verses 5-7, what differences and similarities do you notice?

7. Have you ever experienced times similar to those the psalmist described in verses 16-20? Describe one of those times.

READ PSALM 145:1-12.

8. Describe the differences between this psalm and Psalm 66. What additional truths about God are mentioned in this psalm?

9. In verses 4 and 11-12, what new element of praise do you encounter? What effect can our God-directed worship have on our children and friends?

10. List some of the wonderful works or mighty acts God has performed in your life for which you can praise him.

Read aloud all of Psalm 145, in unison or responsively, as a closing time of praise and worship.

Sing to the Lord

I CHRONICLES 15:1-3,11-28; 16:1-36

*After theology, there is nothing that can be
placed on a level with music. It drives out the
devil and makes people cheerful. It is a gift that
God gave to birds and to [humans].*

—MARTIN LUTHER

M usic seems to be everywhere—at the mall, in the dentist's
office, in the car, at the grocery store, even in elevators.
But this kind of music isn't necessarily meant to be noticed. It's
"wall music"—just part of the background. But what about
the music in church? Is it just "wall music," too, added only to
set the mood? As we watch King David prepare for worship,
we'll take a closer look at music and how it enriches worship.

1. What difference does music make in your times of
worship?

READ 1 CHRONICLES 15:1-3,11-28.

✐ 2. What did David do after he had finished building his palace?

3. What role did the Levites have?

✐ 4. According to verses 16-28, what festive elements are mentioned? What qualities would these elements contribute to the project of moving the ark?

READ 1 CHRONICLES 16:1-6.

✐ 5. What arrangements did David make for the ark in verse 1? What additional arrangements did he make in verses 4-6?

Read 1 Chronicles 16:7-36.

6. What truths about God did David emphasize in
these verses?

7. Why would *singing* these truths at this event be
important?

8. In 2 Chronicles 5 we read that David's son, Solomon, brought the ark of the Lord's covenant to the
temple in Jerusalem at a later date. Considering the
contents of the ark, what does the treatment and
handling of the ark in these passages imply about
the importance of the God's Word?

9. What do we do in our worship services to express these truths about the importance of the Bible?

10. Imagine your church worship services without music. How would this change the service? What qualities would be missing?

11. How does the music in your church vary from week to week? Does it sometimes reflect special events or days? If so, how?

Take time to worship the Lord by singing a hymn or a praise song together.

At God's Table

I CORINTHIANS 10:14-22; 11:17-34

*It is...called Holy Communion because when
feeding at this implausible table, Christians
believe that they are communing with the
Holy One himself.... They are also, of course,
communing with each other. To eat any meal
together is to meet at the level of our most
basic need. It is hard to preserve your dignity
with butter on your chin or to keep distance
when asking for the tomato ketchup.*

—FREDERICK BUECHNER,

Wishful Thinking

ymbolic actions such as the Lord's Supper are rich with
meaning and have a real effect on our lives. How we
approach the Communion table affects our worship and our
relationships with each other. In this first written account of
the Lord's Supper, Paul dealt with some problems in the
Corinthian church and offered clues about what it means to
commune with God.

1. Think of a special meal you have had with a friend or a recent Thanksgiving dinner with your family. What was it about *eating* together that made the occasion special?

Read 1 Corinthians 10:14-22.

2. How does Paul describe the Communion cup in verse 16? How is his description of the bread similar to that of the cup? How is it different?

3. What is the main result of sharing the cup and the bread (verse 16)?

 4. What did Paul say about the loaf that indicates our relationship to each other (verse 17)?

 5. In verse 14 Paul warned his readers about idolatry. According to verses 19-21, why would it be wrong to join in a meal with a friend if some of the food had been sacrificed to an idol? What might God's response be (verse 22)?

 6. What are some ways we might spoil our participation in the Lord's Supper today by our involvement with the world and its "idols"?

READ 1 CORINTHIANS 11:17-34.

7. What problem came up at the Lord's Supper in the church at Corinth? What was the cause of this problem? How did it affect members of the church (verses 17-22)?

8. Have you experienced similar kinds of divisions at your church? What effect did this have on the people?

9. According to verses 23-24, what four things did Jesus do with the bread? Where do you find these four things in a contemporary Communion service?

🖉 10. Earlier we read that the bread and wine are a participation in both Christ's death and each other's lives. What else does the Lord's Supper involve (verses 24-26)?

11. In verse 29, what did Paul mean by the words "recognizing the body of the Lord"? What impact would this recognition have on the problem described in verses 18-22?

12. How does the Lord's Supper enrich worship, both personally and corporately?

13. Summarize what these passages have taught you about the meaning of the Lord's Supper. What do you need to change or strengthen in your own life as a result of these new insights?

Family Celebrations

LUKE 1:57-80

The birth of a child in the Jewish community is an event filled with great joy and a keen sense of responsibility. As in all facets of Jewish life, the covenant with God is the prime concern when a new member is born into the community, and the "covenant of circumcision" ceremony on the eighth day of the male child's life, usually marks...the special relationship.... The ceremony is followed by a festive meal, often including speeches from the proud grandparents, parents, and the rabbi. Sometimes the father will explain the significance of the [baby's] name during his speech.

—DAVID A. RAUSCH

Building Bridges: Understanding Jews and Judaism

The happy tradition of marking a baby's birth in the Jewish community has a long history. Let's look at how an ancient Jewish family celebrated the birth of a new child and worshiped God together.

1. Describe a recent time of worship in your home. What did you do? Was there a special occasion to celebrate before God, such as the birth of a child?

READ LUKE 1:57-66.

2. Put yourself in the place of Elizabeth's neighbors and relatives. What would you have seen when you went to her home? Why are they joyful (see Luke 1:5-17)?

3. What is our usual reaction to a new baby? In what ways is our reaction different if there has been child-lessness or difficulty with the pregnancy?

4. In verse 59 what dual event occurred? Describe a corresponding event in a contemporary Christian home today.

5. Imagine you are Zechariah. As these events unfold, what feelings would you have at each stage? How might these feelings lead to his response in verse 64?

6. How did neighbors and relatives react to Zechariah's response (verses 65-66)? How do your friends react when you praise God for events in your life?

READ LUKE 1:67-80.

7. How did Zechariah begin his song in verse 68? Compare this opening phrase with Psalm 41:13 and Psalm 72:18. What similarity do you find?

8. For what actions did Zechariah bless God? What do they reveal about God (Luke 1:68-75)? Why did Zechariah concentrate on these actions at a family celebration?

9. Throughout this passage Zechariah quoted phrases from the Psalms and other Old Testament books. What does that tell you about the way he learned to pray and praise God?

How might your prayer and praise be enriched by using the Psalms during your family or personal devotions?

10. What connection did Zechariah make between the truths in verses 68-75 and his own son, John, in verses 76-79? What do you think he might have said to John when he was old enough to understand all this?

In what ways can worship lead to teaching our children about God?

11. Summarize what this passage has taught you about worship with family and friends.

Like a Child

LUKE 2:22-24,41-52; 18:15-17

I do not concern myself with great matters
or things too wonderful for me.
But I have stilled and quieted my soul;
like a weaned child with its mother,
like a weaned child is my soul within me.

—PSALM 131:1-2

When was the last time you were accused of being childish? It's not usually a compliment, is it? As we study what
it is to be *childlike,* perhaps we can lose some of our childish-
ness and regain an open heart toward God in our worship.

1. What do you remember about worshiping God when
    you were in first grade? Write out your favorite mem-
    ory, if you have one, and share it with the group.

READ LUKE 18:15-17.

2. Imagine you are one of the children in this story. What impressions would you have had of the disciples? of Jesus?

3. If you had been one of the parents, how would you have told the story to a friend or to another older child who was not present? What would you have said about Jesus?

4. In verse 16, what did Jesus imply about his relationship to the kingdom of God?

✐ 5. What did Jesus say about children and their relationship to the kingdom?

6. What do you think Jesus meant when he talked about receiving the kingdom of God "like a little child"? How is the children's behavior different from the behavior of their parents and the disciples?

✐ 7. Look at the surrounding stories in Luke 18. How is each person in these sections like—or unlike—a little child?

8. In what sense is worship a way of coming to Jesus? In what ways are children uniquely equipped for worship?

In order to see what may have influenced Jesus' attitude toward children, let's look at his own childhood.

READ LUKE 2:22-24,41-52.

9. Although Jesus probably did not remember this first experience (he was only forty days old), what do you think Mary and Joseph might have told him about it later, thus shaping his sense of the role of children in worship?

10. What did Jesus call the temple (verse 49)? What further clues do you find that he was at home in the temple?

11. What childlike qualities did Jesus display in verses 46-47? Which of these qualities have you noticed in the children you know? Did you have a similar experience of asking adults questions when you were this age?

12. How would Jesus' experience during the Feast of the Passover have led to his questions and his insights? How does your experience in worship lead to new questions and insights about God?

Read Psalm 131 (responsively in a group setting) and meditate on it privately for about ten minutes. Focus especially on the image of the child with its mother as a model for your relationship with God. Then pray "like a child," using simple sentences.

STUDY 10

Meditating Day and Night

MATTHEW 4:1-11; DEUTERONOMY 6:10-19; 8:2-6

*We must come to sacred Scripture ready to be
placed at God's disposal and therefore keen to
hear his Word. This keenness to hear may be
compared to that of a mother for her baby....
Her care affects her senses so that she hears with
new ears. In love of God and keenness to hear from
him we, too, will develop new, inner ears to pick
up his quiet voice, speaking to us words of grace.*

—PETER TOON, *Meditating As a Christian*

Hearing God's gentle voice can be difficult. Listening to
Scripture and meditating on it is one way we can relate
the truths we hear in worship to our daily experiences.

1. When do you find yourself thinking about passages
   of Scripture that you have recently read or heard? In
   what ways does this "meditating" help you?

READ MATTHEW 4:1-11.

2. When the devil arrived on the scene, what had Jesus
   been doing for several weeks? Why do you think the
   devil began to test him at this point?

3. How was the first test suited to the situation? How
   was the devil's strategy linked to Jesus' previous
   experience in Matthew 3:16-17?

4. In Matthew 4:5-10, as the devil continues to test
   Jesus, what patterns from verses 1-4 are repeated?
   How did the devil vary his approach? What truths
   about God did Jesus emphasize in his answers?

5. How did Jesus respond to the devil's bids to tempt him? Why were his answers on target?

READ DEUTERONOMY 6:10-19; 8:2-6.

6. List the parallels you find between these passages and Jesus' experience in Matthew 4:1-11.

🖉 7. If you had been in Jesus' situation—thinking about familiar passages from the Law that had been read during worship in the synagogue—how would the passage in Deuteronomy 8:2-6 encourage you?

8. Write down a passage from Scripture that recently came to mind during a difficult trial or a special moment. How did this passage help you during that experience?

9. How is the Bible read during worship services at your church? What do you do to help yourself remember those readings?

10. In Deuteronomy 6:10-19, Moses reminded the children of Israel of some important lessons God had been teaching them. What major truths are taught in verses 13 and 16?

11. How did Jesus use these two verses to answer the devil in Matthew 4:7-10? What does this suggest to you about the value of knowing Scripture well enough to use it under pressure?

12. What situations can you anticipate this coming week in which one of the verses from Deuteronomy might help you?

The Language of Prayer

EPHESIANS 1:3-23

Uninstructed and untrained, our prayers are something learned by tourists out of a foreign language phrase book: we give thanks at meals, repent of the grosser sins...and ask for occasional guidance. Did we think that prayer was merely a specialized and incidental language to get by on?... Our entire lives are involved. We need fluency in the language of the country we live in.

—EUGENE PETERSON, *Working the Angles*

Whether we are entering God's presence in a large gathering or in private, speaking to God through prayer is an important foundation of worship. Seeing how the apostle Paul prayed can give us some helpful tools to use in talking with God.

1. How does one learn the language of prayer? What models are you using as you frame words to use in God's presence?

READ EPHESIANS 1:3-14.

2. List all the spiritual blessings that Paul mentioned in these verses. What sequence do you notice as Paul elaborates his blessing?

3. What are the Father's actions in verses 3-6? What is his motive in blessing us? What is his goal?

4. In verses 7-12, what phrase or words does Paul repeat that point to the work of Christ? What does Paul say about the Holy Spirit in verses 13-14?

🖎 5. In what two senses does Paul use the word *blessed* in verse 3? (The *New International Version* begins with "Praise be" which can also be translated from the Greek as *blessed.*)

6. Where would you normally expect to hear such an outpouring of praise and blessing? What would you think if you received a letter from a friend that began with such a blessing?

READ EPHESIANS 1:15-23.

7. What similarities do you see between the prayer in verses 15-19 and the blessing in verses 3-14? What differences?

8. What three things did Paul ask God to do for his friends in Ephesus? What will be the outcome when God answers this prayer?

9. What do you usually ask God to do for your friends or for members of your church?

Where do you get ideas for praying (what things to include, what words to use, how to address God, etc.)?

10. What did Paul add to his prayer in verses 19-23? How does this theological narrative strengthen the prayer?

11. What elements of Paul's prayers would you like to incorporate into your own prayers?

A Living Sacrifice

ROMANS 11:25–12:2

*Work is not a nuisance to be avoided. Work is a
gift to be given. Clearly, holiness and work are
not mutually exclusive ideas. Work, on the
contrary, is a necessary part of holiness.*

—JOAN CHITTISTER,

Wisdom Distilled from the Daily

Sometimes a great worship service doesn't translate into a
great week at work. It's as if worship can't make it out the
church door into the street. The apostle Paul, writing to Christians who lived in the capital city of the Roman empire, maintained that all of life is worship and that our lives and work and
play can be offered to God as a living sacrifice. We're going to
discover why and how in this study.

1. Can you worship God while doing the dishes or
    typing a letter? *By* doing these things or *in spite* of
    doing them? Explain your answer.

READ ROMANS 11:25-32.

2. What did Paul say about Israel in verses 25-26?

3. What word, repeated four times in verses 30-32, describes God's attitude and actions towards humans? Refer to Romans 9:15, where this word is linked with another quality. What do these two words tell you about God?

4. What human action, also cited four times, is contrasted with God's action? How does this contrast further define God's character?

READ ROMANS 11:33-36.

✍ 5. What qualities in God's character are singled out in verse 33? In what way is this recital an appropriate response to God's actions in Romans 11:30-32?

6. As Paul continued to praise God, what three questions did he ask? How do these questions enrich the acclamation of verse 33?

7. What phrases in verse 36, expressing the same thought more and more strongly, lead up to the climax of that verse?

8. What is the impact of finding this doxology in the midst of a predominantly doctrinal letter? Have you ever written or received a letter that contained a similar outburst of praise?

READ ROMANS 12:1-2.

9. What did Paul command in verse 1? How does verse 2 help explain what he has in mind? Why do you think Paul said we are to offer our bodies as well as our minds to God?

10. What terms usually used in formal worship settings did Paul use in these verses to reinforce the fact that everyday life also involves worship? How is this kind of worship different from formal worship?

11. What quality of God is named in this passage? In what way did Paul use this characteristic of God to motivate his readers? What else did he say that provides motivation?

12. How does the doxology in Romans 11:33-36 strengthen Paul's appeal in Romans 12:1-2? In what ways can church worship help you face the challenges of Monday through Friday?

13. Name one situation you will face tomorrow in which you can worship God with your mind and body. What will you need to do?

Caught Up to Heaven

REVELATION 4–5

Grant, we pray, Almighty God, that as we
believe your only-begotten Son our Lord Jesus
Christ to have ascended into heaven, so we
may also in heart and mind there ascend, and
with him continually dwell; who lives and
reigns with you and the Holy Spirit,
one God, for ever and ever. Amen.

—*The Book of Common Prayer*

The Bible tells us that, as believers, we belong to the heavenly city. This is especially true when we are at worship on the Lord's Day. We ascend, by the Spirit, into God's presence and, though we cannot see or hear it, join the heavenly throng in praise and worship around God's throne. The building in which we worship may be simple or ornate. What matters is that, in Christ, we are "with him in the heavenly realms" (Ephesians 2:6). Remembering this spiritual reality will enrich our times of worship.

1. When the worship service on Sunday mornings seems merely routine (even boring) and the people around you seem all too ordinary, what can you do to overcome these feelings and give God heartfelt praise?

READ REVELATION 4.

2. What did John see "in the Spirit"? Describe the people, objects, colors, and sounds.

3. What clues are given in verse 2 about the person in the middle of the scene? Who is he? Describe the picture you would paint based on these verses.

4. What does this scene teach you about God, his character, and his works?

5. Describe the worship of the four living creatures and the twenty-four elders (verses 6-11). What aspects of God's character do they praise? In what ways can you follow their example?

READ REVELATION 5:1-10.

6. Who enters the scene, and how did John describe him (verses 6-7)? What question is answered by his action?

7. How do the four creatures and the twenty-four elders respond to him?

READ REVELATION 5:11-14.

🖋 8. What two groups join in the singing? What do you notice about the way John presented the size of the groups?

9. Read through the stanzas of the familiar hymn that follows and underline the phrases that echo—or quote from—Revelation 4 and 5.

Holy, Holy, Holy

Holy, holy, holy! All the saints adore thee,
Casting down their golden crowns around the glassy sea;
Cherubim and seraphim falling down before thee,
Who wert, and art, and evermore shalt be.

Holy, holy, holy! Lord God Almighty!
All thy works shall praise thy name in earth and sky and sea.
Holy, holy, holy! Merciful and mighty!
God in three Persons, blessed Trinity!
—REGINALD HEBER

How does this hymn reinforce the reality seen in these passages?

10. Summarize what the descriptions in this hymn have taught you about God. What have the words and songs of the worshipers in Revelation taught you?

11. What worship principles do you find in this hymn and in the passage from Revelation, especially those that describe ways to worship with the body of Christ?

How will remembering that our worship joins this heavenly worship, even though we cannot see or hear it, make a difference in your church worship this coming Sunday?

Sing "Holy, Holy, Holy" to God as your expression of worship.

Leader's Notes

STUDY 1: PRAISING GOD, OUR DIVINE WARRIOR

Purpose of Study:

- To help group members discern the familiar elements of worship as they are reflected in this psalm.
- To enable members to praise God for his work in their lives.

Question 2. It is important to focus on facts before interpretation and application, so don't rush this stage of the discussion. Future questions will go more quickly if you build carefully here.

Question 3. The imagery in these verses pictures God as a warrior, leading his people, defeating their enemies, and meeting their needs. This metaphor for God appears throughout the Psalms and the rest of the Old Testament.

Question 5. Psalm 68:1,17 recall the triumphal march of God's people from Mount Sinai to Jerusalem (see Numbers 10:33-36). In answer to the second question, the group may suggest Scripture readings, songs that narrate biblical events, the sermon, or personal testimonies.

Question 6. Some ideas: a short praise song after the sermon, a Scripture lesson, or a doxology, either spoken or sung.

Question 12. The list will include Scripture readings, the sermon, acclamations of praise, the procession, anthems, prayers, and songs of praise. This sequence might not "work" because the passage is not a literal account of a worship service. But you could discuss how an understanding of the story of God's work of grace precedes and underlies our ability to worship and how last week's readings and sermon in church, along with our daily devotional times, can prepare us for this week's worship service.

Recommended Reading:

Lewis, C. S. *Reflections on the Psalms.* San Diego: Harcourt Brace Jovanovich, 1958.

Longman, Tremper III. "Our Divine Warrior." In *Bold Love* by Dan B. Allender and Tremper Longman III, 111-33. Colorado Springs: NavPress, 1992.

VanGemeren, Willem A. "Yahweh Is the Divine Warrior." In *The Expositor's Bible Commentary,* Vol. 5, edited by Frank E. Gaebelein, 630-5. Grand Rapids, MI: Zondervan, 1991.

STUDY 2: ABRAM'S ALTARS

Purpose of Study:

- To teach some basic elements of worship.
- To encourage group members to welcome time alone with God.

Question 2. Abram's name was later changed to "Abraham" when God confirmed his covenant with him (see Genesis 17:5).

Question 3. Focus attention on the scant details that suggest loneliness among strangers.

Question 4. God let himself be seen, which is more powerful than speaking.

Question 5. Bethel is in the hills, away from a town. "Call on the name of the Lord" is used in Genesis to mean prayer as well as any other parts of worship that would accompany prayer, like meditation and a sacrifice or offering.

Question 7. Bethel (and later, Hebron) was in the hill country, where population was sparse and nature was a more compelling setting for spiritual sensitivity. Encourage the group to share experiences of quiet times with God in nature.

Recommended Reading:
Nouwen, Henri. *Reaching Out.* New York: Doubleday/Image, 1986.

STUDY 3: THE WORD OF THE LORD

Purpose of Study:
- To show why public reading of the Scriptures is an essential part of a worship service.
- To encourage group members to listen more actively to Scripture readings.

Question 2. Depending on your group, this question could generate a lot of discussion, but try to keep it brief. The point here is that Moses said the words came from God. In this type of Bible study, the aim is to see what the Bible says, even about itself, and not to critique it or to force all members of the group to agree with what it says.

Deuteronomy records three long speeches that Moses gave shortly before his death, summarizing his years of leading the nation of Israel. During that time, Moses wrote the first five books of the Bible, commonly called the Law, or Pentateuch.

Question 3. *Webster's* dictionary defines *fear* as "profound reverence and awe, especially toward God"—in other words, worship.

Question 5. One way to open up this discussion is to ask group members to remember their home when they were in first grade. What did they think about God then? What, if anything, did their parents teach them? First graders are usually open to many impressions, and their ideas are beginning to find verbal expression.

Question 7. Because Moses committed God's words to writing and then gave those writings to the Levites, they have been preserved and proclaimed to millions.

Question 8. It is not clear how much of the Law was read, perhaps only Deuteronomy as a summary. In cultures where people don't own personal copies of the Bible, they will listen to long recitals or readings, during which they can absorb much more than we might imagine.

Question 10. Have the group explore how grand occasions, religious festivals, crowds of friends and relatives, and other important events can leave deep impressions or become turning points in a person's life.

Recommended Reading:
> Old, Hughes Oliphant. "Kerygmatic Doxology." In
> *Themes and Variations for a Christian Doxology:*
> *Some Thoughts on the Theology of Worship,* 41-62.
> Grand Rapids, MI: Eerdmans, 1992.

STUDY 4: WORSHIPING WHEN WE HURT

Purpose of Study:
- To show the group that they can and should worship even when they are sad or discouraged.
- To encourage group members to express sorrow and pain as an act of worship.

Question 9. Zion, one of the hills on which Jerusalem stood, functions here as a symbol for God's kingdom, showing his care for his people, and his rule over them.

Recommended Reading:
> VanGemeren, Willem A. "Zion Theology." In *The Expositor's*
> *Bible Commentary,* Vol. 5, edited by Frank E. Gaebelein, 354-7. Grand Rapids, MI: Zondervan, 1991.

STUDY 5: PSALM PRAISE

Purpose of Study:
- To show how our praise today is a response to God's work of redemption long ago.

- To help group members enjoy using and reading the Psalms more fully.

Question 3. Since we were created as souls with physical bodies, the use of our voices in singing and our bodies in kneeling and bowing makes worship more than a mental process. We can *do* as well as *think* our praise.

Question 4. Exodus 14 recounts the Israelites' departure from Egypt. Psalm 66:8-12 broadens the description from crossing the Red Sea to include their experience in Egypt. In both accounts, God's work of redemption is the topic of praise.

Question 6. Focus attention on *who* benefited in each case *(man* and *me),* the use of personal pronouns, and how the psalmist related the two events.

STUDY 6: SING TO THE LORD

Purpose of Study:
- To learn why and how music strengthens worship.
- To learn to sing with greater freedom and pleasure in God's presence.

Question 2. The ark of the Lord—also called the "ark of the covenant"—was a chest that contained the Ten Commandments. It was originally kept in the holiest place of the tabernacle, and it represented God's presence with his people (see Exodus 25:10-22).

Question 4. The lyre was a small, rectangular instrument having ten strings of equal length, usually plucked. The harp was larger, but still portable, with ten or more strings of graduated lengths. Cymbals were often smaller than ours, and trumpets were made of silver and were long and straight. The ram's horn was exactly that—the horn of a ram—and, like the trumpet, was used for calling the people to worship.

Question 5. The ark was housed in a temporary tent in Jerusalem, the "City of David," while the tabernacle, the official worship tent, was still at Gibeon, five to seven miles northwest of Jerusalem (see 1 Chronicles 16:39).

Recommended Reading:
Eaton, John. "Music and the Psalms." In *The Psalms Come Alive.* Downers Grove, IL: InterVarsity Press, 1984.
Wilson-Dickson, Andrew. *The Story of Christian Music.* Batavia, IL: Lion Publishing, 1992.

Study 7: At God's Table

Purpose of Study:
- To enable group members to understand the real effects of symbolic actions.
- To help members enjoy closer fellowship with the Lord at the next Communion service in which they participate.

Question 4. To "participate" in the blood and body of Christ effectively connects us with him and each other as one body.

Question 6. We see a great contrast between the meaning of sharing a meal at the Lord's Table and the meanings of meal sharing in today's Western world. Business power lunches aim to make political moves or win clients for financial gain. Some eating establishments—extremely expensive restaurants or those that exclude certain groups of people—exist for the purpose of segregating one social class or group from another. If we become molded by these cultural practices, our observance of the Lord's Supper can become hypocritical and its power in our lives can be negated.

Question 7. "When the Lord's Supper was celebrated in the early church, it included a feast or fellowship meal followed by the celebration of Communion. In the church in Corinth, the fellowship meal had become a time when some ate and drank excessively while others went hungry. There was little sharing and caring. This certainly did not demonstrate the unity and love that should characterize the church, nor was it a preparation for Communion. Paul condemned these actions and reminded the church of the real purpose of the Lord's Supper" (*Life Application Bible.* Wheaton, IL: Tyndale House Publishers, 1991, p. 2080).

Question 10. The Lord's Supper is a memorial meal, a visual reminder of Christ's death for believers, and a proclamation of his death even to nonbelievers.

Study 8: Family Celebrations

Purpose of Study:
- To show that family or group celebrations are times of worship as well as great fun.

- To help members see how daily events as well as special events can be opportunities for personal or family worship.

Question 4. Circumcision was the Old Testament sign of membership in the covenant (see Genesis 17:9-14). Baptism is the New Testament sign of covenant membership (see Colossians 2:9-12). For some people today, naming is associated with baptism.

Question 7. These verses are the concluding doxologies to two sections of the Psalter. Zechariah would have been familiar with these phrases from his work as a priest. His experience at public worship shaped his praise at home.

Question 9. Consult a cross-reference Bible for a list of Old Testament passages related to Zechariah's song. Some of the references are quotes and some are paraphrases or allusions.

STUDY 9: LIKE A CHILD

Purpose of Study:
- To gain insight into the qualities children have that help them worship.
- To help members regain a healthy childlikeness in their own worship.

Question 4. The parallel structure of Luke 18:16 implies that coming to Jesus is the same as coming to the kingdom; in a sense, he is the kingdom, or, as with a human king, the kingdom is where he is.

Question 5. We find the phrase "kingdom of God" over thirty times in the book of Luke. The *kingdom of God* describes both the presence of Jesus and the sphere of blessing under the rule of God that he brought through his preaching and miracles.

Question 7. The phrase "like a child" has puzzled many people, partly because they think of childish selfishness, lack of control, and other childish traits. All similes or comparisons are selective: "This situation is like part of that one." Surveying the context will help your group see that Jesus is focusing on the way children will cast themselves on our mercy (like the tax collector), are generous (like the young ruler was not), persist in asking for help (like the blind man), and are quick to change and make amends (like Zacchaeus).

Question 11. If the group seems to focus on Jesus' unusual brilliance, as the teachers at the temple did, encourage them to also think about how normal this kind of interaction and questioning is for a preteen. Jesus is fully human as well as fully God, and we can learn much from his human example.

Recommended Reading:
   Bajema, Edith. *Worship: Not for Adults Only.* Christian
      Reformed Board of Publications, 1990.

STUDY 10: MEDITATING DAY AND NIGHT

Purpose of Study:
   • To see meditation as a continuation of hearing
      the readings at worship services.

- To encourage group members to use Scripture more effectively when they are tested.

Question 2. Although the *New International Version* uses the word *tempted,* the Greek word usually means "tested," which is better here because God initiated the process (Matthew 4:1).

Question 7. Jesus would have heard this passage read every year in the synagogue while he was growing up. Since there were no personal copies of the Bible, people listened very carefully and tended to remember what they heard. Jesus could recall and meditate on passages that paralleled his own experience.

Recommended Reading:
   Toon, Peter. *Meditating As a Christian.* New York: Harper-Collins, 1991.

STUDY 11: THE LANGUAGE OF PRAYER

Purpose of Study:
- To foster prayer based on what the Bible says about God's character and work.
- To encourage members to use biblical prayers as guides, paraphrasing or adapting them to the persons, situations, and needs for which they pray.

Question 5. Webster's New Collegiate Dictionary defines *blessed* as: (1) praise, glorify; speak gratefully of, hold in reverence, and (2) enjoying happiness. Jewish synagogue prayers began with the word *blessed* and were similar to Paul's prayer here, which is a Christian adaptation of the earlier form.

STUDY 12: A LIVING SACRIFICE

Purpose of Study:
- To show how worship extends to all of life.
- To encourage members to worship intentionally in one nonchurch setting soon.

Question 5. The whole puzzle of Romans 9–11 (Israel's place in God's plan) is beyond Paul's understanding, but he knows that God's wisdom and ways are more than enough to cause his mercy to win out.

STUDY 13: CAUGHT UP TO HEAVEN

Purpose of Study:
- To emphasize that believers are part of the heavenly assembly in worship and that there is more happening than what they can see and hear.
- To encourage members to recall this truth as they encounter reminders of it in hymns or other elements of the church service.

Question 8. The numbers grow—four creatures, twenty-four elders, thousands upon thousands of angels, and then every creature—until a glorious climax of praise is reached.

A Seven-Week Cycle for Reading the Psalms

piritual growth will come from a daily reading of the Psalms. Repeating the cycle over and over again will offer us a wealth of insight as well as teach us how to pray and praise God.

A number of approaches may be used. You can read five psalms a day and cover the whole book each month. Or you can read one psalm each week while reading through the entire Bible. The format offered here is a seven-week cycle of psalms based on *The Book of Common Prayer*. The psalms to be read on weekdays are listed in general numerical order, with a portion of Psalm 119 to be read each Wednesday. For the Friday through Sunday readings, specific psalms are listed that follow a death-and-resurrection theme to help you prepare for and celebrate the Lord's Day.

During the next week, choose either the morning or evening psalms for week one, depending on which is the better time of day for you. The Psalms are very rich in meaning, so do not try to be exhaustive in your meditation. Look for one point where a psalm connects with your life and pray about that. In succeeding weeks you will notice more points of connection, but one is enough to get you started.

There are a variety of ways to use the Psalms as prayers. As you read each psalm, you can relate it to the needs and joys of people and organizations on your prayer list. Or perhaps you will want to paraphrase the psalm, turning the truths you find into prayer petitions or praise. Record your meditations in a journal, summarizing your insights or paraphrasing the psalms you encounter each day. In this way you can weave them into the tapestry of your life before God.

Week 1	Morning	Evening
Monday	1–3	4,7
Tuesday	5–6	10–11
Wednesday	119:1-24	12–14
Thursday	18:1-20	18:21-50
Friday	16–17	22
Saturday	20–21	110,116–117
Sunday	146–147	111–113

Week 2	Morning	Evening
Monday	25	9,15
Tuesday	26,28	36,39
Wednesday	38	119:25-48
Thursday	37:1-17	37:18-40
Friday	31	35
Saturday	30,32	42–43
Sunday	148–150	114–115

Week 3	Morning	Evening
Monday	41,52	44
Tuesday	45	47–48
Wednesday	119:49-72	49,53
Thursday	50	59–60
Friday	40,54	51
Saturday	55	138–139
Sunday	63,98	103

Week 4	Morning	Evening
Monday	56–58	64–65
Tuesday	61–62	68
Wednesday	72	119:73-96
Thursday	70–71	74
Friday	69	73
Saturday	75–76	23,27
Sunday	24,29	8,84

Week 5	Morning	Evening
Monday	80	77,79
Tuesday	78:1-39	78:40-72
Wednesday	119:97-120	81–82
Thursday	83	85–86
Friday	88	91–92
Saturday	87,90	136
Sunday	93,96	34

Week 6	Morning	Evening
Monday	89:1-18	89:19-52
Tuesday	97,99–100	94–95
Wednesday	101,109	119:121-144
Thursday	105:1-22	105:23-45
Friday	102	107:1-32
Saturday	107:33-43; 108	33
Sunday	66–67	19,46

Week 7	Morning	Evening
Monday	106:1-18	106:19-48
Tuesday	120–123	124–127
Wednesday	119:145-176	128–130
Thursday	131–133	134–135
Friday	140,142	141,143
Saturday	137,144	104
Sunday	118	145

What Should We Study Next?

T o help your group answer that question, we've listed the Fisherman studyguides by category so you can choose your next study.

TOPICAL STUDIES

Angels by Vinita Hampton Wright

Becoming Women of Purpose by Ruth Haley Barton

Building Your House on the Lord: Marriage and Parenthood by Steve and Dee Brestin

The Creative Heart of God: Living with Imagination by Ruth Goring

Discipleship: The Growing Christian's Lifestyle by James and Martha Reapsome

Doing Justice, Showing Mercy: Christian Actions in Today's World by Vinita Hampton Wright

Encouraging Others: Biblical Models for Caring by Lin Johnson

The End Times: Discovering What the Bible Says by E. Michael Rusten

Examining the Claims of Jesus by Dee Brestin

Friendship: Portraits in God's Family Album by Steve and Dee Brestin

The Fruit of the Spirit: Growing in Christian Character by Stuart Briscoe

Great Doctrines of the Bible by Stephen Board

Great Passages of the Bible by Carol Plueddemann

Great Prayers of the Bible by Carol Plueddemann

Growing Through Life's Challenges by James and Martha
    Reapsome

Guidance & God's Will by Tom and Joan Stark

Heart Renewal: Finding Spiritual Refreshment by Ruth
    Goring

Higher Ground: Steps Toward Christian Maturity by Steve
    and Dee Brestin

*Images of Redemption: God's Unfolding Plan Through the
    Bible* by Ruth Van Reken

Integrity: Character from the Inside Out by Ted Engstrom
    and Robert Larson

Lifestyle Priorities by John White

Marriage: Learning from Couples in Scripture by R. Paul
    and Gail Stevens

Miracles by Robbie Castleman

One Body, One Spirit: Building Relationships in the Church
    by Dale and Sandy Larsen

The Parables of Jesus by Gladys Hunt

Parenting with Purpose and Grace by Alice Fryling

Prayer: Discovering What the Bible Says by Timothy Jones
    and Jill Zook-Jones

The Prophets: God's Truth Tellers by Vinita Hampton
    Wright

Proverbs and Parables: God's Wisdom for Living by Dee
    Brestin

Satisfying Work: Christian Living from Nine to Five
    by R. Paul Stevens and Gerry Schoberg

Senior Saints: Growing Older in God's Family by James and
    Martha Reapsome

The Sermon on the Mount: The God Who Understands Me
by Gladys Hunt
Spiritual Gifts by Karen Dockrey
Spiritual Hunger: Filling Your Deepest Longings by Jim and
Carol Plueddemann
A Spiritual Legacy: Faith for the Next Generation by Chuck
and Winnie Christensen
Spiritual Warfare by A. Scott Moreau
The Ten Commandments: God's Rules for Living by Stuart
Briscoe
Ultimate Hope for Changing Times by Dale and Sandy
Larsen
Who Is God? by David P. Seemuth
Who Is Jesus? In His Own Words by Ruth Van Reken
Who Is the Holy Spirit? by Barbara Knuckles and Ruth Van
Reken
Wisdom for Today's Woman: Insights from Esther by Poppy
Smith
Witnesses to All the World: God's Heart for the Nations
by Jim and Carol Plueddemann
Women at Midlife: Embracing the Challenges by Jeanie
Miley
Worship: Discovering What Scripture Says by Larry Sibley

BIBLE BOOK STUDIES

Genesis: Walking with God by Margaret Fromer and
Sharrel Keyes
Exodus: God Our Deliverer by Dale and Sandy Larsen
Ezra and Nehemiah: A Time to Rebuild by James Reapsome

(For Esther, see Topical Studies, *Wisdom for Today's Woman*)
Job: Trusting Through Trials by Ron Klug
Psalms: A Guide to Prayer and Praise by Ron Klug
Proverbs: Wisdom That Works by Vinita Hampton Wright
Ecclesiastes: A Time for Everything by Stephen Board
Jeremiah: The Man and His Message by James Reapsome
Jonah, Habakkuk, and Malachi: Living Responsibly
   by Margaret Fromer and Sharrel Keyes
Matthew: People of the Kingdom by Larry Sibley
Mark: God in Action by Chuck and Winnie Christensen
Luke: Following Jesus by Sharrel Keyes
John: The Living Word by Whitney Kuniholm
Acts 1–12: God Moves in the Early Church by Chuck and
   Winnie Christensen
Acts 13–28, see *Paul* under Character Studies
Romans: The Christian Story by James Reapsome
1 Corinthians: Problems and Solutions in a Growing Church
   by Charles and Ann Hummel
Strengthened to Serve: 2 Corinthians by Jim and Carol
   Plueddemann
Galatians, Titus, and Philemon: Freedom in Christ
   by Whitney Kuniholm
Ephesians: Living in God's Household by Robert Baylis
Philippians: God's Guide to Joy by Ron Klug
Colossians: Focus on Christ by Luci Shaw
Letters to the Thessalonians by Margaret Fromer and Sharrel
   Keyes
Letters to Timothy: Discipleship in Action by Margaret
   Fromer and Sharrel Keyes
Hebrews: Foundations for Faith by Gladys Hunt
James: Faith in Action by Chuck and Winnie Christensen

1 and 2 Peter, Jude: Called for a Purpose by Steve and Dee
Brestin

How Should a Christian Live? 1, 2, and 3 John by Dee
Brestin

Revelation: The Lamb Who Is a Lion by Gladys Hunt

BIBLE CHARACTER STUDIES

Abraham: Model of Faith by James Reapsome

David: Man After God's Own Heart by Robbie Castleman

Elijah: Obedience in a Threatening World by Robbie
Castleman

Great People of the Bible by Carol Plueddemann

King David: Trusting God for a Lifetime by Robbie
Castleman

Men Like Us: Ordinary Men, Extraordinary God by Paul
Heidebrecht and Ted Scheuermann

Moses: Encountering God by Greg Asimakoupoulos

Paul: Thirteenth Apostle (Acts 13–28) by Chuck and
Winnie Christensen

Women Like Us: Wisdom for Today's Issues by Ruth Haley
Barton

Women Who Achieved for God by Winnie Christensen

Women Who Believed God by Winnie Christensen